INTERNET
GIRLS

poems by

JSA Lowe

Finishing Line Press
Georgetown, Kentucky

INTERNET
GIRLS

Publisher: Leah Huete de Maines

Editor: Christen Kincaid

Cover Art: Leah Gardner

Author Photo: C. A. Stamper

Order online: www.finishinglinepress.com
                also available on amazon.com

Author inquiries and mail orders:
Finishing Line Press
P. O. Box 1626
Georgetown, Kentucky 40324
U. S. A.

Table of Contents

for A

She looked up out of her voice and saw the angel.
The angel who says, "It's time."

"Is it time?" she asked. "Does it hurt?"
He will have the most beautiful face she has ever seen.

"Oh, babe," the angel starts to cry.
"You can't imagine."

—Denis Johnson

Run, little nightjar. Run and I will hunt you.

—Whit Merule

I.

You can put back anything but dust, dust is eloquent

Blister & filth.

we were poets at the end of the world and every night I
grew toward what it would be like to die, I was not

in love with anyone. for every thing that is cobalt, that
sure is a lot of things. sand sifted in soft drifts like snow

when I walked the shoreline, still your widow, shelling.
we were missionaries in the field, played griot, cantor,

we told it, we wrote it in script on the surf-wet beach,
said it into the salt sea with our hands, it was only

witchcraft. obviously no one listened or scried. I spoke
a few words when we met, *meat*, *chew*, and *sadness*:

you learned me *careful* at first, then later *rage*, *lies*,
even your face schooled in untruth, its various tells.

my inabilities at poker sieved justice away. we unwrapped
warm paper from a kilo of tortillas de maiz, más rico.

that was the holy day when I first teetered, slid askew.
we held a speakeasy, uncorked the viscous chardonnay

before its time. now I eat plangency, drink plain
water; wake into the grateful morning glad to be

alone, have no one angry with me, no one's mood
spilling like bloody paint outside the frame. when I

think more on how the cat died I get this crawl feeling,
go to hands and knees around the floors, mouth

open, keen. I found three stiff whiskers, her black
high gloss. having forgotten which partner it was

who would always cough while falling asleep, I grew
limp and emptied, I was not in love with anyone, we

were the last poets left at the close of the carbon era,
dazed by information, wordy, supposed, unremanded, it

was the end of the world, we were right
down in it, we were not lost—,

A needle of sapphires & thieves.

There must be a mistake, you don't come visit
me, people don't, I visit people, that's how it works, who
live in more interesting cities, I choose cities what never

freeze, refuse to move where winter can't keep palm trees,
and you are you, that young; so there is definitely an error
or escape. I should wash my hair more, count scabs. The

sores number as in exes or times I've scrambled to throw
the cat in the carrier—once blind psychotic, walking in her
dish, now bleeding out across the new lavender fleece

blanket, drooling urine so frightening arterial red that I
ran them, justified. The traffic lights. But might have done
anyway because the rule is: don't scare passengers, but

when I go alone I barely notice, I drive like I don't want
to live, I do and I don't, you don't know, it's complicated.
The friend who dumps me thinks I'm alcoholic, the one

who picks me back up again after a year, I'm an old stone
or little object on her dresser, that postcard altar we all had
when we still sent them. Just a petite chose pour souvenir,

that's fair, I don't dare read his emails and what happened
to me was not all that bad. If I had screaming nightmares it
might make sense. Mediocre abuse means mediocre wounds,

so nothing that dramatic. The trapeze angel died of heart
disease at 45, this could be my last three months. See, I'm
actually good with that. I've known a lot of love, and given

some. They'll forgive me in an urn. I was always the reason
I couldn't have nice things and that includes, what, your gift:
tiny feather on a necklace that I continually lip, mouth at, run

over my teeth and tongue as chain and charm go bronze
from skin and saliva, it's been a fabulous party, I've tried every
drink, now clutch at different dressmakers, urgent: thank

you, here, I'm done with this, will you please have it back now—

The lesson.

You can lose a moon: when almost nothing, already the least pale
visible line then the airplane banks. It's gone, it comes back, I want to
show someone next to me but he's texting so it winds up being my
strange moon, mine not shared

with you. She did the thing, we marvel and approved: gave up
dairy grain sugar wheat coffee chocolate alcohol all animals. It
was like her weight fell onto me, motionless, uncleansed, and I
deserved it so l took it. Thicked.

Quicken the rank discovery that even double-chinned, fallen
breasts, rolls along the ribcage, she still persists, the want of touch.
I slot in car keys to shock: I'm mom in the driver's window. Well I love my
mother. And the one who under-

stood yet jettisoned me (awake all night on the sofa while I lay wild
and fretted in bed) rose back up into her beauty, queen of pearl-dove,
a sheen of dignity and true quiet I'm not even sure she'd recognize,
she lets me to fester in my parables and

lies (bent over a filing box, shoving in dusty VHS cassettes as fast
as is safe for the final divvy, the friend-divorce; oh look, there's her
name, playing at a club I used to peer orphanly in its windows; dry
up, shush crying by the time they arrive)

(she didn't need to know about it either, just if only just if one just
one square of self-respect is left) (it's left) like this: she maybe threw
it away or it snapped, symbolic, the black-white-red plastic anklet
I beaded her during occupational

therapy. If anyone needed to keep track of misspent hundreds it
should have been me, it's not generous if it's desperate, just stupid.
Two years in there's still a stitch. Try to drag in a breath, hitch, knit,
knelt on the tile coughlaughing,

press your hands to the site, no water mixed. Keep it in. So you got
a friend in your few years here to vehemently agree the eponymous

record is the only one we really need. If a gift, it's pitch: stumblerun through gasps on packed sand and when she

catches up to mind repeatedly, byronic and stunning, tonguelash letting me have it, dash out faster, scrape fingers through salt hair to shake past wrath, shells crunched under heelstrike. I can't fix or outfox myself, could never dig out that stab.

When I was little my mom (in chase of livestock) slid down a gully side and fell. In slick-soled gumboots; shorts. A stob of some old weed, fibrous, broken-off shank, shot deep into her thigh, could not be stitched so left its silvered crater. Why,

I carry counterparts. Consider a clip, shove-clicked into magazine, discharged at paper target torsos, clustered tight in center mass as each bears a woman's name, I never said I was original. They can't take tape or staple, that rich contempt,

deliberate slick withdrawn. Lifted herself up direct off the stalk and left her glob of fat and meat behind. We wouldn't seek to be loved, not in the first place. But it's the shove back, flinch, to leave one dumped. Lessened: glued to stay. And in

every way: obviated: always the pallbearer, never the bride.

Guttersnipe.

It's her in the picture: barn jacket, library entrance,
all waifish eyes and hair, I asked her for it but she would
not give. Now the dog lies down in shallow water

to cool his belly, blow bubbles, stoned on Trazodone
because he's scared of thunder. We walk so slowly,
his tufty feet slosh in puddles, he has no ideas, not

about adhesive leaf-scurf caught in feathers, his bag of
scumber I carry, that the pelt of rain on human skin feels
bare, unwelcome, bad. Its visceral pull to shelter. I

tell myself to soak it down. *X is dead* they said earlier
and for a weird moment I thought it was my ex
but it was another poet: terminal, a new book cover,

his wife, such meals and laughter and work still ahead.
They all go into the dark autofills my mind and I tell it
to shut off. I just have nouns, nothing doing. One

seagull cruises down the cut valley of the residential
street, not flapping its wings. Whatever else we
assumed, one of us was to be stationed at the death

of the other. Her linen handkerchief with its echidna. My
literary executor; my three quilts, my two fake daughters.
We can forgive each other every kind of stuttered thing.

She's my boyfriend.

Sorrow barrows into chests, makes its home, refuses
to hibernate, we borrow cupsful as the therapist
moves the tissue box back and forth tireless from
one rachel to the other, no idea what happened
to their babies only that they now simply are not.

Touched my hornet's nest so nimbly yet persistently
I took notice, kept offering yourself until I saw
what this one was: husbanded but wildlife, all cheekbone
green-eyed, wise prose to remander an assassinated
man beloved. That shamed, closeted character, I

had to realize, was me. Or both of us. Then I turned
bower-bird to press my shabby gifts upon you, junky
tinsel, old foil wrappers, gilt beads,—and you full married,
an Atlantic away. Twenty years ago was her, in her tiny
denim shorts and halter top. A market where we walked

too nervous to hold hands, a man asked "do you have
a boyfriend." She looked at him dumb, unable to say the truth:
she's my boyfriend. The arbitrary is the crutch of the tragic.
I lullabye you with a starry indigo wish—for sleep to pull
you under, cradled by my own sewn quilt into exhaustion,

tugged by the low foghorn's 3 a.m. blow. Another one won't
come, I am used to never being used to it. Frozen in a clutch,
what is my dire take-home, none: only yesterday a pop
song started me like a stag from the brush, I had to pull off
the interstate to finish or not-cry, could have just changed

the station but weeping fails to keep her, antlered, alive—

More than one apricot.

she said, simply: because l am soft & lovely. and l
agreed: there is nothing wrong with you, a phrase
your sponsor taught me. no this is not for you. she
hiked back to her waist, shining skin & knowledge
she does not need that "honesty" to fix or better
what's always been fine to start with. sets out
every morning at seven on her loop path in these
foothills to joy, sun purpling snow, a movement
not exercise but communion, hiking as prayer or
church with feet, remember my teacher hobbled
gamely down from the ski basin with a shattered
anklebone. pain made up of non-pain elements:
heat, tension, weight, pressure, sharpness, twists.
like I can write our romance using just my mouth.
"like when you allow" she said "yourself, to have
more than one apricot." like it climbs up all alone.
when you more nearly nestle, sift curious fingers
through hair she'll show you fractures, fell colors
that in all your long masochistic enslavement to
the violence you keep calling honesty you may
have likely (piñon pollen choirstall) not yet seen.

Sequin.

something   luminous   sheets off one woman

    dark   wraps   another
                                in   an   ache to

        take you to the desert   live
            hard   right   clean   as long
as possible

            merciful virgins
forgive themselves   all who travel past
            (the long vigil)

            start over

    •

        ten men lovers
                no one left   alive

                                white
    shadows   wet
    sculpture   your nightgown
            blame me
            thinking you real

                                rich endearments
    (you were real)

        artichoke heart
        asparagus spear   melting
        avocado flesh

            mobile knees
    wide-eyed animal cries

your little dowry   butter
                    glee

•

                    christ   unface her

        curling around   broken open next
to   night body

                turn
away
                        face the dark   stories

        some old things still left to be
    said

                no guarantee

                who gets to say them

•

                    dovetail

                        open doorway
                bathroom tile   gleam pink
                    swing   wire brim
                    toiletries   tipped fingers
                watch them nearly

    fall out   scented washes and rinses and oils

        light falls   a square less clear

cold stalls   dried shower   less

come by your room some
time

the light
little basket   only promise

you could never   not promise

•

morning
                              drowsy
chemistry   overhead light buzz
dim head   nod   like
poppies   heavy with seed
                                        folded
wings rustle   silvery paper
sift down   brush fast   that oblivious girl
                    behind you

trail crumbs   an ice

this planet dislikes
romantics

men   cannot fly   and so shoot birds

•

                              pure siren color
line   so much   gauze   sharpened

gentled   ragged   to petals

sea-pebbles   hungering
              for clarity   to swell

              you   never
would
                              in the meantime

an infirmary   could

        wounds
                    stand in   for   all   fullness
        a body might hollow

        worn liquid   out of shell

      if beauty held   an answer
                              none came

    •

              can't ever
change   the scent
                    warm lemon
taste
                                          wanted
        to tell   woke you

(apology)
                              glimpses
                              made nervous

too perfect   then   limn tropical fish
        watercolor pencils   dowse   aqua
turquoise   lime

                        nursed
        emerge blinking

scarved   lack of sleep   rambled in salt

submarine

•

valences
alkalinity   ion rotation
kept awake   someone used   to   inside
blossoms' music   pay

attention   don't   punished
punished
punish in turn   pique

stamps   tiny feet   fled   frustration in
a new boy   dread her hurt

inward

inconsolable

•

just   walk
across the graveyard
resume effort
an halting task
next your movements

some time or other   try to be
try to cut you
out of this skin   try a year then

put you back in careful ink
place

the winter   we
hoped for

perfect

two halves   fit close   give off

a nearly identical

quiet glow

II.

One beats and beats for that which one believes

Dear analogous beloved, or poem,

You are still not listening. I said, contradict my syntax! Come on don't be that way, come on now.

I said I want you to bend over and pick up the spilled matches; you look at me with your eyes full of thumbtacks.

I want you to bristle with diction and your fur is like milk.

When I push your head down, your body convulses in a sight gag—hack, yack.

You are such a doll, I moan, seconds before I accidentally knock you in the jaw with my elbow and your nose starts to bleed. This is our gory sitch.

You use that meek *okay* of yours like a church key, it could open things. Why don't you.

There's not much time, I've been pleading to your rosebud mouth—say *Chicxulub crater*, say *impact extinction event* or *K-T boundary*—

You sneak around the house, I am causelessly irritate. I always, you never. You always never.

Don't be so pretty. More protean. Don't be—

In your dream I tried to saw at your throat with an electric carving knife. I don't know why you would dream that.

In my dream my mother bought you a set of Revere Ware and you moved out anyway.

You pocketed my shocked quartz. I had to play online poker for hours. Of course there were others. Say *thermodynamic equilibrium*, say heat death.

I lied to spare your feelings. I didn't throw you into the cenote. When you were sick I gave you ginger ale, I gave you credence.

What did you want from me, that I didn't eventually serve. I mean, give. I mean, take.

Embroidered sorites.

I.
Sentences landmines.
There is almost nothing I can say. When I say almost nothing, even worse.
We walk gingerly they still find my feet.
I just ate a pomegranate Greek yoghurt, but not decently.
You got me every time.
Anyone who thinks she can be trusted with a sentence is innocent.
Tsvetaeva said, "No one has taken away anything." She said, "I savor our separateness."
I wanted to say, *I don't know which idiotic outburst you mean.*
Some books must be read immediately and without pausing, such as *Tristram Shandy.*
We are no longer allowed literary allusions. Or matinées.
I wanted to say, *But your hand-grenades are never idiotic.*
My lips are red and chapped from forgetting to drink water.
It is not possible that you are fifty.
Nor I terra incognita, even in solidarity.
Innocence did not therefore mean that I am allowed to cause pain twice.
The bulk of what goes unwritten lies beneath sand, not ticking.
I wanted to say, *My lip would bleed right now if I bit down on it.*
Your preference is for figs, not wives.
Not foreseeing why metaphors, and violent ones, would soon be required.
All this happened despite *The Anatomy of Melancholy.*
Why would anyone offer other women live ordnance.
No one who can believe in our former belief in innocence, is in the least unholy.

II.

If the woman told the truth about her life, a world would split open.

But the question is, *Which one.*

A monastery is the least-safe place you can think of. We called it the knife room.

Verbiage, persiflage, superfluous; as opposed to completely and permeably sympathetic.

Thinking against myself like a weapon, *I won't ever see Rome.*

In trying to list red flags one could grow abashed, discommode even oneself.

So what has led to strange men biting my fingertips at 4 am in a cabin in California.

Dying childless or penniless as long as not American or unpublished.

In half-sleep, jerking off the edge of a stair step and encountering air.

At its tip a milky round bead, literal white quartz.

Anything I am capable of calling a "warning sign" cannot therefore be one.

Handling every household object with the half-thought of thrift stores.

Circumscription is not an idle threat, usually occupying about three years.

Plants are less mobile than animals, according to your botany textbook.

It was okay not to have one as long as I had books, or Italy.

Rare fish drown in tanks thanks to our gray neglect. Thick water.

As closed off to me as the possibility of a daughter.

Trusting to such safeguards as being old, unattractive, or married has proven ineffective.

Propinquity is not a padlock.

Things I know how to do include: lie, omit, take myself to movies, throw out my neck.

Also: write, triangulate, twine intimate epistolary tendrils.

I couldn't help myself, we say.

Historically descriptive, if not morally excusable.

What does "trying" look like.

It is apparently possible (we know this) to do things you don't know how to do.

A lake can be hypereutrophic and (eventually, up all night talking but not to you) dead.

Diegetic.

To brood in a cool bath,
imagine all virginal as when a child,

tangle of one single hair calligraphic against hip,
pubic thatch grown
thicket, bracken, no access to that
because I think we broke it, compromised inside as I have never
been, rearranged in some
intractable way like cracked-open ribs or -ectomy,
unbridled Bardot part hacked off
not coming back. And for this you have not

borne the mend, or how could you, sloppy auteur sloughing off
amid a welter of half-truth and shabby excuse,
girlish arguments that made no
sense or how could they, because *no*
is not an incomplete sentence; only plain guilt compelled
those garbled explanations, managing
another damage, what you mangled where it could

have been a cut cut. And all I have to say about
that (drying off bubble-soaped thighs) is look, every
night the cat stretches up toward the bathtub's
skylight, her thoughts so single you can
read them, eyes blown
all pupil: *sky window!*
sky window I will climb, I will climb up
to it—she looks around wild for purchase

and finding none, cries, angry, angled by desire.

Beatitude.

Just as the shower-pipe drip rusts around the drain
into a blue-green copper-encrusted calcium ring
rimed with hard water, salted like a lime rind, so

the ugly plumbing runnels through this can
track and channel who we have become, back
down into who did it, started it, when. Though

common doctrine prevents our going there, as if
entrails themselves forbade us to look under manhole
covers or peer inside weedy culverts. We're no longer

those same dears, they're dead and (presumably)
gone, disconnected from us or any wiry current
events, no puzzling out the steps from there to

here. So now, tabulae rasae, we, okay, give up:
how to deputize our ancient twisted karma, our
bitternesses, cloacal and blackened, to obsidian

grins. Yes, these are chestnuts that are not very
interesting, the apophthegm that people in pain
refract the world to others, revel in revealing it,

that in Southwestern cities whose airstrips have
names like Sky Harbor and Sunport I should bite
at you, whoever you are, to feel that stupid old

something-anything; again bromidic, as if blunt
sensation were as good as—which, come to speak
of it, perhaps it might be. Or better. Why not

admit things. Make space within the convention,
for what, I forget; for whatever, for that for which this space
is reserved: for the bedlamite or the lunatic (as once we

delegated what we now make sick) that they might
be love's carriers, picking up all the shit that gets
laid down and doubled in the course of a daily

average, the wet stuff no one would touch with a
pitchfork; fire up your torches but someone has to sleep
with politicians, be a starfucker, do your dirty

service, this work of being soap-slimed and broken.

Request.

Please I am holding very still and still holding in one
hand an organic poptart. Please let this still be not.
Please she is not weeping into the receiver, please,
please this doesn't happen, you will unhappen it.
Please I still have to feed the cat and she is crying.
Please do not make me hang up and drive to her,
not whispering at the cars on the freeway, please
undo this dying you have made be here now please.
Please some of us are standing in an uncertain circle,
some of us fall silent and staring at the floor,
some ones of us suddenly sob, suddenly stop,
please none of us know what to do with our faces.
Please these are not your last poems left now, please
you leave us all voicemails in which you say you are
feeling better, so please feel better now, talk to us
now, please leave more long voicemails that get cut off;
be riding your bike, you are riding it to us, you are
on your way now so please will you spare us your love.
Please be losing your temper again, please just climb
the mountain, any size, please keep trying to climb,
we will all be keeping trying, please help me sweep
the hardwood floor and work on my bookcases with me
and sweep up the sawdust, please will you come over now,
please it is all so late at night and our eyes are washed red.
Please our uncomfortable laughter, it is only because you
should be with us, standing quietly back from the fire and
cracking open a beer. Please come here, will you just please
not be so stubborn just this once and come over here.

Love song for Rachel.

1.

her rain.
          Poured from a saucepan
(how could she not have known)

(at her dan tien or
hara
a nest of twigs

)—then a startle, the robin comes
crackling out of the branches

2.

As if it were a cute little town or toy
village we pretend-inhabited

her eyes swollen almost
shut from crying
voice a thin threat, something about
a rope—

what we pick up we pick up, hold
fast to, move
          on it—

3.

There is a part in every
day like this, the desperate flight
reflected in rain boots,
unlimited class ashtanga pass, her

hair home-dyed glossy chocolate

I start to think of my car as a machine
that plays music, of my house

as a box that holds kombucha, a place
where plants
                    come to die—

4.

Crocheting in a cubicle
with fair-minded sardonic hope
of no reprieve

I want to buy her, be her, give her
my dinner, take
hers, cut up her mango, proffer salad
leaves with bare fingers

(as if hands could anything
as substantial as
a man)

5.

it was a dull length of pipe or a gun
muzzle, it was urban
decayed

Feeding a bird she knits
to holiness

curve
curve

she has nothing
her beautiful everywhere
you could eat it

6.

An overcast hour slavish with gratitude
a drink hurts your throat
a cream
a sweet to sit in your lap

(snowflaking, the drishti is at
                          your feet—)

a sprouted green thing, perhaps an oat

& no one's eyes should be that full, blue
set in a heart-shaped face like

gems. Or eggs in a nest—

Tares.

1.
Plummet plunge under October. Now just as dark. The walk.
She is only among a relentless present now she eats her own
heart in the marketplace. Will all men say 'What' to her. Talaq,
talaq, talaq: She makes him say it aloud, looks straight in his face.

2.
Vervain, verbena, vetiver. My brocade, my drop of India;
my sisters, the slovenly needlewomen. Yes, jezebels make
the best seamstresses. Daydreaming, sneaking help from the
patient-fingered when necessary, and often this is necessary.

Needle tipped with rouge, a loose woman. Coal-black on a
pinhead lines an undereye—smoke, sooty sting. She says roundly
in her head: my clientele are my own business. She would
say it aloud if he were there. Sick of a sudden. Don't think it.

But she must: the abattoirs, the blue cigar, the crush of the auction
and that male voice babbling, unravelling livestock into
cuts of meat while they stumble uncertainly from their pens,
blind with fear, uncertain of exit/entrance, uncertain of all

but stink and lost. The baby. Where it was. Not anywhere, they
can't. And her mother had laughed, and slapped the mare
hard on her sweat-streaked flank. Not now, she won't.

Please mourn the roses, all of them. Every one.

3.
She knows he will be cold,
where he goes tonight.
She knows this because
she made his coat herself.
The best (again) because she
has ripped out Bible pages

and basted them thin to its
flame-red worsted lining,
then in turn sewed that
tight shut with the black
bias tape. Turn the collar,
last longer. Buttonholes
ragged but sewn through.
The ones who dressed
in Chinese silk and sang
at the robbers' campfire.
Any sister of soprano injuries,
these are the ones to trust
with your greatcoat, but
do not wonder that it cannot
protect you, where you go.

4.
I'm going to write a song:
bluebird, another bird,
another bird and *another*
bird and then a chorus
in Latin. I'm going to decipher
the sign in my favor. You
can only breach blue
with a poetry.

5.
I begin with little premeditation, only a fluttering image
of a grass-covered green burial mound in summertime,
sempiternal: it is a barrow, that is the name of it, there is

a sensation of below the grass, earth; and below the earth,
bones. And you and I lie entwined in the layers, either
on the grass or half in the soil, joining it companionably,

what we are not permitted in this life, and in high desert
there is no grass anyway, only wiry clumps strutted among

the greebles of rock and grit. Now I will tell you, because

you will understand: the difference, between earth which
is whole and huge, sound and round and profound; and soil
which is rich and edible, a dark cream to skim and chew

and swallow down. Somewhere you are reading Fortinbras
or Laertes, you would be a perfect Horatio, deceptively
mild yet strategically brilliant; and dirt, which is what you find

grainy and particulate in your drawers after a slide into second
or a hard fall from the tree limb, begrimed along the back waist-
line of my jeans on your way home afterwards, marked

and scarred, as a kiss burns forever into a palm, as we get in
trouble for all the plastic cowboys in our pants, hastily wiping
it away, to hope to remove, that is, the streak of my cerebral

lipstick scarlet and marred; and finally dust, which everyone
knows lies soft collected under the bed. And hushed. A little
dead, like ashes, a little shurred or tired. Like an old flashlight.

He is no longer underfoot. And if she understood my master's
lissome glove removed, you have unhanded me, could feel
the bite of my pillow, could hear my weak scream through

the rolled-up car windows, would she worry less. I know

6.
I would. Never your face at the blinds like a small warm star.

III.

I went out full, but empty has G-d returned me

Internet girls.

she loves me not me not she maybe never loved me do
I begin to track to square it away can I put words to the
void of it fill the shape walk automatic to and fro made
of space more holes than here more gaps than matter
the poet told me it's so important to have my female
friends oh yes I said she went on so that we may lie
together and give each other naked massages with
scented oils and whatever my face did in that moment
was apparently the right thing because she went on
blithely oh look my grandmother did not make it to
eighty would wake at four a.m. to set a pan of hot rolls
brushed with sweet milk as the train diminished other
side of the sorghum field where pesticide droplets
bitter liquid I spat clear into the grass kept me and my
cousin lulled in our thick sleep she was my first
internet girl there have been dozens since then she
said *I've finally got you where I want you* in that box of
ash and grit he doesn't want me to say I wake in the
night with barbs of her rusted nail shoved through my
child's wrist but listen I will tell you all of her least true names

MÆRE

black wax splatters on institutional flecked tile spell out
a pentagram on the sabbath she plays bartók on vinyl
charcoals crows on paper reads sexton gets her first
period in our cold beige bathroom stalls outside which I
crouch to reassure to give instructions for cardboard
tampons I fail her I fail to understand fail to care she
weeps in fear later footsoles dusty that she may fall
unconscious on her back drown like poor jimi hendrix in
ungainly vomit I know nothing (her long hair) only
dimly get this an intensely gifted six feet adopted from
the dinétah we lie and roll her on her side tell her to fall
back to sleep so lost in my own stupidity cover for it
hoping to front to pass with my long virgin braid and
flickering brain in greek we learn the word for fate
μοῖρα learn in physics to submerge lead and tin crowns I
learn to insert a diaphragm slick with jelly to dance
alone to stand between two men to abandon myself she
became action an untrammelled bell housebound
daemon became bright fire a lapful of violets to shriek at
me in allcaps let go her hand fail to understand I fail

MICHEL

her face poised intense above her father's old green
raincoat silvered elegance with a cigarette case out of
time we play-skate on thick pond ice above frozen koi
her hand hot and dry in mine she scatters sparks waltz
in a lavish arc of loveliness silken black hair I play
whisper-fiddle on its scattered strings in morning dark
she comes to me her brother having shot his head off
her body heavy in my numb arms consolation is zeno's
never allowed never to eat away what hurts I lack the
man to stab his heart in a trickle-down market can only
dance only show words we scream at each other in a
public street I have kept every paper letter littered with
proto-emoji *dearest kira* I have kept every weary listen
broke vodka tonics into endurance whatever was spoilt
confused *if you love me then why are you so angry* my
russian wedding dress bloodied in lacy snow I thought
this raven girl would close me she climbed triumphant
up the front range married well became her unflawed
railroad her own noir nib to pen herself an architect of
structure and ordinance marbled thus never to be held

KATERI

grey gauze scarf an incense a mess of soft henna blur
a ham sandwich dried in the sheets a bent pen he was
always there *for showing me what love* is until I locked
doors threw contents of drawers cut deep as I dared
with a tiny Israel army knife's castration blade slept
with the guitar in the bed she loved it not me trailed
after them in paris and london *l'autre femme ma poule*
saved every blue letter when words turned insectoid
repelled reading even others even when married went
back to her helpless as fog curls hand to wave
her face in the train window saltwater taste of her still
on my fingers in the dark she woke to let in the cat
came back dark chocolate in her mouth did what she
wanted when the decade let up her earrings didn't
fluster me warmth of her thighs pink satin ribboning
taut a taste sweet like musty hay the truth walked into
me jetlagged I collided full body with concrete bollard
bruises intense down my shins for days if I had it to do
again would I beg eternal return drop my head on her
shoulder dazed under a north star actually I did

ALLION

any baby wombat any otter what were we supposed to
she was my gulf waffle I am going out and may not be
back for some time as we know healthy bodies throw
off constellations of symptoms I don't want to be brave
here is my little pen here are your men here is your
kombucha mother and the one who throws his laptop
here is your gris nuage and poussière de lune here my
long letter written all night in teastains and arabic here
is a bösendorfer missing keys plant your fey garden in
pruned anxiety I cannot soothe paint watercolour grids
blue on blue squares smoke and brouillard move wafty
speak repetitive can I miss that wild girl of ecoterrorist
yurts that maid marian corseted on the trading floor
she reads all of woolf the one shape she admires wave I
go back to buy plated hydrangeas gone yellow petals
called between her calves in starlight her high cries her
mannered bow yet the need to die in her arms as my
blonde amazon godsister crawled up into the bed lay
with her head on maman's chest and listened to the last
few (long spaces in between each) faint heartbeats

ROSY

blackpudlian in a wine-dark gown pools at her white
throat in our college underground down bailey's cream
whiskey shots for £1 billiards portishead>pulp>blur>
we scrape off the edges of bridges get lost in fields of
golden rape walk miles on new year's on the edge of
the irish sea slush-salt rimes my doc martens why I left
wildflowers with neruda outside her sporting oak door
I knew better jane frowned always mouth before mind
before she mattered we lay heads in a circle laphroig
nina simone diamanda galás butter skirt black tights
my bumblebee we crept into the upper common room
to leave a painting she seemed so much older with her
scarves and plummy rp yet we outlived her breasts her
professorship weaving great fraudulent theses out of
my guts you led me under fairy lights through its time
grassy meadows sheep stones stiles a lighthouse face
splattered in woolf's violet fountain pen ink *I think
I know my type and it isn't you* screams until her voice
breaks dolores is gone now too breezy's welsh tales
who was this yank to think I worthed your lily intellect

MAREN

don't talk to me for awhile so I didn't the [cracked]
dust of plaster in mouth my own fault for being useless
bad uterus not to cast out [embryo] clung instead four
needles deep in the cervix she's at the bar being loved
a dip of tobacco a twist of slim waist seventeen [my
cleïs] sundresses [   ] no one knows [none] what I hid
on the inside of one raw thigh [name that scar] after
her climb through its jagged pinch to scream out another car window protestors gather to denounce [it
feels] [right] miscarriaged rough drag of [hemp rope]
her binding or bandage deftly she's hoisted lifted aloft
to spin filigree clamps of butterfly metal kink to nipple
there is that we [are not] allowed half [daughter] half
witch half exultant prince[ss] which rippling knights me
I serve to burn to kneel [thick] troubadour minus lute
knew no better no cascade of hair no auburn mind her
desired shimmer-sentence clomb wingéd from the first
mint-green page I [kicked into love] as a tomboy throw
up like a [beginner] that's how she knew I shall kill who
ever dare touch one single [cell] of her soft loveliness

CLARISA

I live where roaches fly you in a cold metal sleep of air
you run steppes an oval ice lake as you lace them but
 still do with a baby and husband written on your face all
cheekbone and mess of grass-eyed shadows how do
your novel stalks grow you slink tall across stage boards
he didn't know he also left you when a'hanged himself
 kissed both dogs on the mouth left us both isn't it
strange how I still hang around here nothing to fix me
except your moment I thought you desired me paled it
flew back barefeeted through old snow striae
gold urine red lithium cry to dream I again bottlecaps
cigarette butts your chin narrow by mine skin bared in
the sanitarium would you then have me madness linear
interior your mother only forty did you understudy any
lunar or linguistic slum the frou you wrap around all
feather its foxtails in a vague of cologne or petalled lip
matte her I ever coveted in a touch withdrawn draws us
along behind it long legs in your rhythm unworthy
nothing of me allures your slip your elegant sentenced
let me finish no one need get hurt all satin all plethora

JULES

your second album stuck inside the cd player of my car
is not a metaphor I touched your hair recoiled in horror
at myself sheer number of times I fuck-upped a celesta
pulling clean sheets onto my bed your tight corkscrew
coils acoustic piano catsick dried onto hardwood your
articulate money and tiny square of dark chocolate all I
wanted was for you to like me all you want was a black
lipstick in the end I give you flattened cardboard boxes
brush off the silverfish lie *have a date* to watch the red
headlights wink out like a migraine at the end of street
when I asked *why do you walk so slowly* what I meant
as queenly any philopater intestate beaten left to gild
glide whether orgeat or moscato tall as her gentleman
all regal scamper behind ever your troll now your hour
falls peaceful as leathery petals from unblushed bough
flesh-pink cabinets I repaired on my back as we sang
bad pop sticky-papered plaid their roachy insides you
vow *don't let them take away your phil collins* installed a
window unit uninstalled accidentally brushing your tit
in the dark one last thing I could give you: wide silence

OLYA

we're supposed to have brunch to translate the birches
still growing inside her heart her river frozen enough to
skate on her scuffed white bootlets move I pick her out
of the party first she will be mine know just the russian
poet's name to call her immediately by her diminutive
shows me her caesarean scar my test cuts nine high on
a thigh an inner wrist named for her dark chatoyant as a
cat eyes always intense vibrating my name knows
instantly something is wrong drags me out to the pond
where I meekly spoon cold potato soup confess I have
fallen pregnant and everyone I love is furious at me for
my carelessness she will drink 2 bottles of champagne
mock me for choosing bisexuality be shocked when I
can read Мастер и Маргарита but anyone could I argue
we argue prosciutto and vodka in the freezer she'll ask
me to stay but under the orange soviet sodium street
lamps what it won't mean always drives me away I sing
in my car while clear moonlight has her way with me
down the dark stairwell my bra and one sock in my
purse she'll text when she wakes up and I am not there

ROWEN

à droit de seigneur nothing I say will keep you from
fucking him nor a scarf wound around her throat stop
rape when I held you air held still pizzicato-plucked out
of time insane すみません you stole up behind women
in street-length furs to stroke them fingers all charcoaled
taper where streak you now where do you slip aside
settled meticulously picking stitches of your red fox quilt
to read woolf underneath painting blued grids in braided
dragon breath grey a glittered dance to make my dulled
life strange without you *she's my boyfriend* our flame
gutters the slow pour of infernal dirt covers its face why
keep my book but not my bones I will buy wheat-free
tamari pasture butter promise to meet any devils in their
plucked ring of bluebells lost in prairie grass took you to
see bunnies to be arrested in bikinis praise kittens being
professional cats go to the window to door to see what
the ruckus someone touched your house take your hair
down from its mahogany hashi a wiry silver curtain
speak the one language we invented or let him know I
loved you first and longest and worst

LAURIE

cloaked you arrive by glide *alta l'acqua dell'arno* sleep
on a park bench le zanzare puncture skin you couldn't
believe your contempt could stop my mouth but does
a really premature letter multimodal notebooks to
burn you carried me to my own bed where we sat
down all bewilder unsure what to do next I liked her
too much to betray another of myself liquid not at all
solid can you accused me of constellations when I but
hide in plain sight wear a black watch scarf to protect
my only soul from me not your fault not knowing our
code you never bled through your lucky batgirl
knickers never were catcalled never endured an
unwanted tongue in its hurry andrea wasn't wrong we
each encounter an assault the two of us crossing st.
francis all but holding hands his vituperative letter
fireplaced no need to read it more than once sylvia
wasn't wrong her vaulted nails her droop and cigarette
the purple letter disappeared by a jealous other would
I have driven out to meet you as far as the blue
swallow possibly for I was one unable to resist mystery
or command and sex her tallest order

LEAH

wordless I always fell you so meticulous violin scales
precisely placed apostrophe for a 'cellist whatever I
offer was not enough the bleakest place to live virginia
said a mother is to want and want and never to have
would not curse anyone such your coruscating wings
cerulean your buttered jonquils dead red anatomically
correct heart chambered why did I never catch joy for
that I love many people and change my prince often did
I queer half of our sons your rules for play an arrow so
confining I cannot mate in captivity someone else was
my fox my emerald in the snow lack of patience to
blame but I never meant you harm clutter up the tag
she said deleting social media is a suicide letting anon
scream just hands them the razor and says go on cut we
were child prodigies how do you recover from that in
our long lives it excuses all crimes I am humid super-
saturated sodden with empathy rules of pray marked
on the court like a narrow lane so then why send me a
wild violet swimmer on turquoise why my typewriter or
broke sewing machine why paint me your over our foe

trained crazy ladies on closed course the nights I spent
arguing for hours with your animus the razors of his
satanic eyeteeth I should have known when you gave
me a coffee mug with your therapist's name on it still I
was still lying still surprised when you cut me free claim
it was for your own survival did you find someone else
to argue down the devil find someone else to tell you
about your genius worthy of walking on this earth and
breathing our air I kept that cup but covered the name
with a sticker I kept the sushi toy but try not to look at it
what will you do when she dies or worse than falls
pregnant what will you do when the police blotter says
the fire is at your door what will you do when you run
out of college courses I would have married you and
taken you to the desert the ocean the marais le midi
instead left you with a silver bowl in your lap for vomit I
hope someone holds your head I hope you are at peace
with god whoever you conceive her I hope you find a
place to put all your language variegated vinous warped
wrapped my wet ankles wild vertiginous freed

RAE

deep ukraine her necklace of red velvet tied its knot
around my ceiling fan would dance every weekend at
your wedding you wobbling in her chair far above our
heads your blonde husband and his matching brothers
matched shot for shot I ordered single-malt at the bar
then lay awake all night to talk novels with groomsmen
now childed you too him too all of you reproduced I
post a bisexual rainbow tutu tiny nirvana baseball shirt
realize I'm turning your infant into myself ca. 1993 in
lieu of having you on my lap drinking from my brandy
alexander I wove down the curved hotel hallways after
laughed how every decade stays the same the years I
could only come thinking of your breasts from out here
a shift between registers sounds effortless but maybe
from inside there's the little blue mermaid toy caught
in your throat a sharp pain when you go from chest to
head no such thing as over our workshop hydrangeas
grated nutmeg sacks one reality was I watched the last
episode first and sat tear-soaked in your living room
wondering who was that woman? for whom I wept?

KAT

any young mother in black-and-white on a hardwood
floor coonhound and a mason jar filled with clear liquid
you are the warmest cigarette ember my variable star
my equinoctial waters given heft placed within ten
fetlocks or a held arm's distance keeping him out a full-
time job would you never neither without the width of a
hem would you rather be comforted by waistlines or
kilted skirts above full-breasted I dove under the water
to grasp its hook through my cheek slip off wet garotte
granite clotheslined by your easy grace to confess love
true as quilts my scots-irish grandma was stood on the
back porch dusted in corn pollen her fogged outline in
the wet of dawn an augmented chord you knew this lemon
set with black pins selvage cut with pinking shears a load of
laundry warshed and wrenched you would have lived this
with me forty years ago now all left to send you are these
nine-patched postage stamps hopscotch ticking tacked
sweet salt hay faint greens and arkansas roses why you
left is less important than that you did

SOFIA

two years until I heard your singing voice a spring-soft
miracle then I knew what those cheekbones and arch
of mouth had always been for vibrant wood sounding
board she said it *turns the whole house into a speaker*
that's how orchestras vitalize no microphone always in
its right place told you a secret told you my lie for you
lying in blueing which is it your deep curve under my
clavicle we write each other in but one degree to the
left disguised by wing-grooming (clay dish of warmed
olive oil) by pirate by seraph would anyone be tricked
into salt disbelief when it bells out this clear my cousin
would only kiss me with a white jewelry box between
our lips the meaning of which came uncertain to me
we bathed slept fought like feral cats together her long
dark hair in my fist white skin between my teeth the
only love I knew when I repeat myself you can be sure
that's you when comfort scuds away like low-slung
clotted fog that's a form of cloud made landfall were
you to agree if we became selkie no apex predator to
complete a male triangle just wet just right just you.

LUCIE

I keep thinking how I wish I were a poet to describe things
certain things I cannot get right like crane flies redbuds
butter-yellow pollen thick on a pickup truck windshield every
morning the lilac tree with its grape- sugar hanging flowers so
sweet it scrapes the back of my throat raw like vomit you
died last year in february but every time I try to say so it flops
immediately into this stupid elegiac second-person voice
"you died last year" like motherfucker she knows that and
I've literally been walking the dog and trying to write about
you and this goddamn tree for over a year now you must be
somewhere shaking your head over what a disaster I turned
out to be all inelegance wadded and no diction all scaffolding
and nothing to do with the sharp reality of things with that
mango a blow job your thighs in exercise tights flanked by
maine coon cats like library lions blue cigarette in your hand
you should have lived twenty more years books grown old
enough to spurn them all derisive your toys superior your
method the only one and I still betray it

SHILA

you know what I think you think I'm fine I think you
think I'm better than fine I think that's what you need
to think in order to keep ignoring me in the greeting
card aisle picking out one for her doubled over to my
knees both hands on my gut realizing *she's going to
have his baby* a new bottle of pine-green fountain pen
 ink its color relief not to worry unbroken bough of
serenity another whale-dark another powdered dust of
a moon are you aware every novel I write is openly for
you if you're happy I can bear anything if you are safe
now if all the losses were to prepare me for this pitiless
white absence that has sucked all the wet magic out of
 life did you think I wouldn't notice that it wouldn't hurt
that there wouldn't be a gaping bone socket if I could
stoop to the raw spring I would if the bucket didn't hit
well bottom in a dry puddle of mud if you care about
the cracks at least tell me you're joyful don't let this
last be for nothing to let your hair down its harsh burnt
leaves scent or vegetable in a vanishing blued smoke at
least let him hold you house you make you at home

SAM

what word ends only that over more came when what
if I've started smoking again lying picking absconding
illegal vanilla cigarettes an ear filled with fresh lymph
so I play the same radiohead song over and over and
over gouging my finger in the wound but why not they
keep on coming they're not going to stop I forge an
interest in oldest fruits bell peppers rabbits metal soil
paper clips running water indecisively indented paper
I get to say how it was for me that's what's allotted nor
allowed if I've only three years left I'm not going to not
say all my life I've believed I had her as a friend when I
was four a little girl with my name I called her on the
avocado phone was she not real was she not imagine a
little girl dreamt her wild hair bonfired red a little girl
knelt in gravel with another tangled towhead chalked
on a rock heart I LOVE YOU to remember each other
what if all this time she was my imaginary friend what
if when I have to google to find you how I know it's over
over it's over it's over it's over it's over it's over it's over
it's over it's over it's over it's over it's over it's over it's—

IV.

Nothing left remarkable beneath the visiting moon

Contraflow.

Insufficient libations, and to the wrong gods. Almost always the culprit.
A Sig Sauer and a Glock. With a handgun, you have to take aim
and shoot, it's not like an automatic, you can't just fire into a crowd.
Garden of kinder, our child-flowers, in the parking lot I watch a strange
woman waving enthusiastically to a baby who blinks and waves back, are we
    not filled
with something? If not love then love, the entire species focused on our most
vulnerable (aim and shoot) but let's not get off point, can we not admit that
    three
dozen dead, some children, many children, is considered a good day's work for a
drone pilot. One .223-caliber rifle kept in the trunk of a car. Your narrow waist.
The dialectic of enoughness which exceeds adequacy, the narratives of scarcity,
how complex and how luscious that complexity; how painful and vital. My
right palm smells sweet, like a handjob, like cunt and saliva, like when you
drop off, breathe in soft jerks, drowse, your laptop's hum low. I pull up the duvet
protectively, I am not going to love anyone but if I did it would be. Outside,
banana plants and palm trees, our street's landscaping invisible to passers-by.
    No.
With a handgun you have to point, it's not like an automatic, you can't just fire.
Almost always the culprit. Insufficient libations, and to all the wrong gods.

An epistemology.

There's a part of me that *doesn't* want to die,
Part that wants all pretty things to be forever, nailpolish to sparkle
         with points like gold stars,
There's a part of me that circles "2" & then crosses that out & circles "8,"
A part that circles & both the numbers tell just the one story,
Another part worships these chubby bees wrestling open each tiny coneflower,
There's a part of me that tells the voices, *Stop it,*
A part in this courtyard knows the difference between ego-syntonic and -dystonic,
         knows enough to get up & lift someone's sodden forgotten kalanchoe
         out of the dirty cold water in which it's just sitting rotting,
There's a part sneezes with mouth open so little shreds of red grapeskin scatter,
There's a part of me that keeps dying every time, that
         dies when I sever my hands at the wrist with a saw, cut through
         the church of bone and offer them to some invisible pitiless one,
There's a part that's been devoured, & the hungry demon finally satisfied,
A drowned part, a frozen part, part poison & part asphyxiate twice,
A part talking all the time, telling itself funny stories when no one is listening, song
         & dance, shuck &
         jive, variety, vaudeville, working its shtick,
There's a part that doesn't care,
I don't care, there's a part that bitterly regrets,
There's a part that can't go on from all that it remembers, the worst parts, its ugly
attempts,
A part that wants me dead, it plots & tries,
There are parts, these parts, these are all parts,
There's a part to point out the slow drift of a buzzard riding her thermal, headed
our way,
         not a hawk, unflapping, better look alive,
There's a part just now as it fell up, yes into the sky, away fastly from all this,
There's a blue part that's always rushing upward

For Cleïs.

To me, she appeared

And I didn't expect
to be punched in the chest. Love is [
] a memoir of
vomit and rosewater [   ]

Her flat voice [ ] the phone, *I'm going into* [
] *the hospital* [
] its smell, gray-flecked [
eggs, plastic mattress cover, leaving [

] the door open
] bathroom
] just, she speaks and my stomach
falls to my ankles

Something [   ] dark grabs my [
and twists them, my
mouth is suddenly dry and I have
no [   ] in my body

Daughter-friend, younger
poet, I've left all of my
[   ] to you when I die, my [
]

] And I thought *is this love*, dazed [
] sickness [
] rinsing over me as I stood [
] cold outside [

my institutional door
blank [
] humid [ ] and in
] then [
                    ] shivering [

Operation soul retrieval.

Look, it doesn't appear—it seems to not be—we don't think
it's going very well. If the soul is a whorled coil, a cochlear shape
in the center of the abdomen, a blue-green curl behind the bile
duct, somewhere, then all is well; but otherwise we feel a real
concern that you have not got this more under control. We
worry, frankly, about the unfollowed narratives. You needed
to something, is our consensus, and failed to do it. To lean
over the edge of the pink sofa arm quick and firm, give her a
stubbled cheek kiss, does such a gesture really pull the soul back
into the body after all her months away? Especially with this cold
rain, days of it, and no warmed adobe walls to draw her home?
When she can't feel her feet. When she can't even see the moon.
That, contrary to Californians and Klonopin, joy should be fugitive
after a certain age. That anyone's chest would froth with corrosive
bitterness, black and flaked like the oil pan from an old pickup truck.
Cups of tea aren't doing it. Or moping around the house holding
a tiny Kwan Yin figurine curled in your palm like a roll of quarters
in case you need to punch someone. We know how dumb it hurts.
We know you wake every morning in a state of lack, we are well
aware that before your eyes even open you feel insufficient all the way
to the brainstem. We all know you've been running on fumes & charm
for perhaps a decade. It is what it is, to have failed her. And we want
to tell you: it's not so much that she needs to listen to the gods, it's that
you'd better make her talk back. These same mornings, a plain line
of sun glances toward the beds, makes translucent the pretty lettuces.
Tell her about this, urgently; don't just remind her about the time
you accidentally drove into Wales, and everything was greener
than green could have been, with bright red phone boxes in another
language—but promise you'll take her back there. Make claims
you can't support, agreements or liaisons impossible to keep.
A soul wants hope. A soul clambers down striped slits of light
through thin clouds in order to believe herself needed here.
Undivorce, repatriate, reconcile, solicit. Stock up on syntax
and semiotic coin, monger her loyalty with words if you have to.
Her warm skin can candle yours again. Her breath, her breast.
Inside your body lit up like rupestral figures of ochre, granitic
thighs and spears, the pulse of running beasts. You can do this. Yes.

Virgin painkillers.

Love spent the night with you and your deepest self is raising a terrible racket.
   —Carlos Drummond de Andrade

One of those times. Worn out like a toddler. The cat ecstatic that
I have come out to her house, to her office. She writhes in the dirt
under the wooden bench as I sit limply and drink. The fey are they
who you see only out of the corners of your eyes, damp rags,
little bits of shadow that drip more than flicker. The park, I discover,
is filled with bats at night. They are fey too. It's time to admit

I'm completely crazy, it's what will kill me. One part cream
of coconut, which really means sugar, four parts grapefruit juice,
a cup of ice, no rum because of lithium, and "don't even bother
making it if you don't have the nutmeg" so for five dollars I made
sure I had the nutmeg. It's devastating how savings get frittered,
fripperied away. I don't know how one trapeze cashmere cardigan

eats cash; but then there's the crazy, the trip to Japan, the new used
car, the saving the cat's life with four, five trips to the vet. Alertly she
looks out into the dark, loud male voices drinking beer, not nearby
so she is not too worried. And I am alcohol-free, my brain is free,
I cannot seem to make plans or think how I am going to get out
of this mess, in my old Cambridge market dress, black with roses on,

so instead walk mindlessly out into the grass, the round place where?
where months ago in the car on the way to teach class I saw a ring
of huge white puffballs, as if they had been dancing while I wildly slept.

Endemic.

dear joyful,

the blue crane whose mate was shot dead
lived alone for years on our lake
from then until now
a long stripe of steel gray in your hair
I ran too much current, too hot
through the copper coils wrapped around our core
that then snapped like a spine, ash incinerate
if the last gift you want is this one, that I should stay
away from you
you know by now I will give it

•

dear fifty-one,

never have I been the adult to wear a wrist-
watch, my godmother said *why would*
I strap a timepiece to my body
like a bomb
the head intestate makes ceaseless lists while the eyes
swerve, all I care about now is the pelican
adrift, folding its wings against
a shredded lane of the shipping channel's wet
ink there was only ever one
last place to hide

dear foxglove,

paper masks litter the gutters, I can't find
an unwrinkled selfie angle
wake in the night airless compress and say aloud *am
I dying* but it's just
heartburn, I want to cut back, do less
but if I do less won't I then
do less
she's drinking a clear green South African
chenin blanc from an open-mouthed jar whereas I:
loathly, contained, risible

•

dear lockdown,

libido-throttled I make tonight's bad decision
to drive, sex like vomit crowds my
throat my breastbone like you could rip up a rotted stump
by its roots
do you crunch through xmas trees longing for forest
see how HARM glows inside PHARMACY
get called sir in flannel, stare into the child's face
you will never see again in this
life she put me inside her bottle but the lid is gone
and I still don't leave

dear fixie,

as if her own heart had
fled her, for some of us life was never normal
I dream your husband drags me away to serial-kill me
huddled dull on the floor of his chainsaw safehouse ask only
will it hurt much and *how long does it take*
now buy coconut milk tea, boba an extra 50¢
clearly someone up and died because on the
beach a small crowd
lets go a cloud of Mylar balloons to drift
out over the open sea

•

dear subtle findings,

they dye your eye
with iodine at which point I realize I'm disabled but aggressively,
half-mocking, already defensive and snobby
probably put everyone off me
from the moment I opened my extra mouth
then wondered why they were so prickly, insistent on staying
estranged from myself, like that time
like the five bottles of wine on her
living room floor, four girls adored I thought I was
making friends

dear scratched cornea,

it's not you, it's uveitis from when the dog clocked
the orbit of my socket while we fought for the toy
steroid drops make bitterness
skip the back of my throat, I bend to spit
in the sink, think
did you miss any piece of this or is it just a
relief to have it gone
torn up, cancelled, jubilee debt, student loan
forgiveness, popped moscato, meantime I can still map
every sky-blue cell of your skin

•

dear mistress,

took after a bad habit of hammering nails into my own
hand, accentual syllabic, never knew
true rain came down in tones
lip the cool flat of her wax seal I pretend
the christmas card's romantic
like the time I tripped on carpet into a student's arms
(sinewy, warm) we both recoiled
his wrists wreathed
in blue tattoos I'm alright with my fight
fine by my fears and my queers and my tangles

dear ice storm,

gilt plastic beads clack against wrought iron
beach empty of krewes. in
the twelfth month of quarantine we all struggle but
mine has been thirteen. marry
an epidemiologist and change your life
yet we could not live with blood-hunger, parish widower
gas lamps gutter porches, a mantilla. you
know I am doing wrong and so do
I can any glaze or gauze
stop it up

Syncope.

I love you, I love you is what we say
but only when we come, the foam
of the coffee is sweeter than the bitter

milk, *I am not a well writer* my student
wrote sadly in his self-evaluation, there are
mornings I look in the mirror and say this

to myself, hoarse with sleep: *I am not a well
writer,* I don't know how to get better?
books I don't read, days I leave work

as soon as I legally can, evenings I plan
to go running or do yoga, instead
camp on the sofa, video games, wine, *I*

am not a well writer, frozen pizza, sex,
the classy kind, with eggplant and goat cheese
and maybe salad with bright-

burst cherry tomatoes, tart balsamic, greens
to make us virtuous, a Calvinistic
form of election, vegetation, *not a well*

writer but this won't last forever, they'll
be my books on my shelf, name on spine,
I will get sharper in the mornings, I learn

to drink coffee, will read Deleuze & Guattari,
I will circle and define, finish half-started
essays, think past P to Q, understand Quine;

come further home, not just the brief lull when you
loll on my collarbone, know it will not last, I am
meant for alone, *I am not a well*

writer, not a mother, never to have a child;
and I have no bible of work, no book nor blood
and this body is only mine tonight—

V.

And I shall be dumped where the weed decays;
and the rest is rust and stardust

In which she makes mistakes by the Mississippi.

1. on canal at chartres
that's where we first stood (soft), not anywhere
you would think people would stand, to find other people,
maybe to watch from the most awkward place possible:
hot sidewalk in front
of our conference hotel and them shoving past, a child
held twin red and blue balloons longer than he was
tall, untied animals or maybe he just couldn't wait, needed
to grab two colors in each hand, both of us laugh
but I could not have said (we were soft)
why
     (her colors: rose-salmon startled lips, wisteria draped
blouse, folds dipped into decolleté; we drank pimm's cup, light
tea rust-liqueur with cucumber slices. I, abashed
       for my ragged
untrimmed hair, raw cuticles, strange heavy post-
hospital body, took it into the bathroom to put pink lipstick on it
at the very least, where l promptly dropped it and shattered on the
floor; so instead, stupid with nerves for days, calmed by
reading stall graffiti:
   the cult starts here
you are all butterflies
and YOU CAN NEVER HAVE TOO MANY ANGELS,—which, not
entirely sure about that last one)
until she said clearly, l heard
it: "I'm glad I met you," genuine, precise; we agreed next year's
drinks would be on her, I never saw her again. a strange thing
happened then, no,   two.

2. down st. ann to decatur
in the drugstore l stood with my chin resting on a metal shelf
to stare blank-minded, why, I don't know, at a small glass bottle
whose label read REAL GATOR TOOTH so obviously, owing at least
the same sincerity in return, I text
you looked beautiful tonight
before I buy a bottle of water and drank enough to dump a packet

of raspberry lemonade vitamin powder;
with it like a flask in my pocket
of the borrowed rain coat, wove down through the quarter
swigging, everyone veering away like I was tipsy, sung my
(tired hoarse soprano, what happened to me, confused, new,
how was I got this old, homely, plain) cover of "moon over bourbon
street," since I'm where I can, a city with every smell: beignets,
gin, vomit, weed, hurricanes, burnt praline, trash,
and sit down hard on concrete blocks, bladder swollen, watch the full
actual moon full on full waves from a barge, chill inside this coat, in
as usual love with everyone.

3. woldenberg park
     but that song has hard intervals.
the last verse covers five registers. and if you don't know this about
me
(like I love finding scratchy salty seaweed in the polka-dot
top of my bikini much later after the beach; or, I went en pointe until
my feet broke so that's how you wear heels: turn off all feeling below your
ankles; or, even as my drunk hookup tried and tried, mumbled what parts
of me he intended to fuck, he stayed
a doughy two-incher, which, I
didn't honestly mind, my mind wandering to her throat the way minds
do) it's that I always have
something to say, unfuckingshutuppable—"this
cow not for sale!" a girl behind me shrieklaughs, to her date
or whoever he is—and when whiskey-dick fumbled
a clumsy hand through my hair I flinched, waiting to be
hit in the face, and held my breath to take it;
faked it
for the first time in my life, or three out of five, him too gone
to hear me yelp in abraided pain. had to show up to give a paper scraped
raw inside and pissed off next morning, rolling my eyes at myself;
when it was over, he stared sightless (blackout)
(dumped by wife and girlfriend) at me and said: *that didn't help. you*
aren't helping. sobbed hot and harsh onto my collarbone, so I tried to give
him what I had, and listen:
you can never
help.

4. paddlewheeler creole queen
thus, in conclusion, it's a river, very big, and the air
comes off it so cold my hands start to shake, pianist fingers once
slim now swollen, no one tells you hand shapes change as you age, this
isn't a revelation or anything, but twist and look,
    back: just a moon, okay, you don't
have to deserve it, pretend to come, you can lean against a guttering
iron lamppost whose gas just gave out, someone says to no one under one *did
you*
hear, the moon will be red at four in the morning. but me, child
of a guitar player and a stewardess, I heard. she won't even read it,
is probably asleep, appreciative of sedatives—which, that's when
she texts back, polite friend: *thank you! travel well.*
so I'm out here with rats and train
tracks, men yelling rough at each other *faggot*, you died and I'm
alive for this ink water, alive to be older. there goes a quiet
riverboat, pooling dark collected, dragged behind. I'll be alive
for chicory in the morning until I stop propositioning girls
or give up, run a maternal hand through his boozy hair, accept my new
invisible; I had that married interlocutor who reassured me
you'll be fine,
you always are, such laughably awful
reasoning: of course I'll be alive until, well, something else. so
you're welcome. so thank me later.
this is my nickel train-smashed at the crossing guard, these
are cotillion girls in heels picking their anguished tiny path on cross-
ties and blunt chunk gravel, this is my fresh
pointless wetness
and him, young enthusiast, introducing me to his mom; this is
a block of text in eyeliner in that same bathroom:

I loved my friend so much I hoped for more (she said no)s

so I loved on, a desperate believer,
divider: three parts in vain but two
just here for the river.

Dear za'atar,

Intermediary, I loll in bed at 3 pm and eat raspberries. Not much longer now. While you are across the Atlantic trying to scratch out of your skin, seraphic, molten wax, heat- feathered and muffled, do they hear you scream (tit pic, eczema). That you think of me as harmless is my privilege. Cheek roughened red from sleep against the pillow slip, nothing is okay, forty days in a room, nothing will be, I know your tubercular wedding tastes, I know enough to know (eau de nil, celadon) what is not for me (monkhood, a child, reciprocity). I can be calm. When the porn star comes (daughter of the Buddhist priest) she reaches up to draw down, kiss her lover (with her face still slick). We seek to connect in all our trials. In the movie when the world ends, she says urgent to the driver *Let me out here, I need to be with my family.* Who is yours, little shatterbolt, little ibis, egret, ushabti, blue cinnamon, phoenix, quasar, ripple of light, soprano prism, harmonics, overtones, rainstorm, blurred rapier, inbox I abuse, advantage I take, luck I push, little foxfire, phos- phorescence, gleamed dreamer, driven, impatient to be photons, little redolence, glazed tanzanite, prosecco in a slipper, poisoned thorn, ball lightning, little outrage, little maze?

Pyrrhic.

Now that there's nothing left of you but a bankrupt casino, all the dinettes
and red leatherette chairs for sale, now you write things like This sounds like
a threat but I assure you is not, followed by a really scary one, somewhere
around the time you lavishly said *You deserve to die in a fire*, not going quite so
far as to name the one who might set it—

                              I stop here, chop lacinato kale and sweet potatoes.
In addition to my tiny sharp gold-bladed sewing scissors, you seem to have
    made
off with the vegetable scrubber too, so I use a Brillo pad. Does this count, am I
blaming you? Because you cannot endure any blame. It must be
displaced.   Even my most verbal female friends never
want to have meta-conversations, whenever our closeness ruptures they wait a
time, passing, a reliquary, I acquiesce to a slow closing over, then we resume as
if ignorable,

which is not a word, and I try to be cool about all of this, I do. I did. But my
girlfriends only break my heart, unlike what your mathematical countering
took:
        sometimes I'm allergic in spring, and when I suck the snot back
down my throat, salty across the soft palate, abruptly I feel afraid and dismayed,
why? it's a flashback to semen, could that ever be for someone else a happy
memory, what things are happy:
                          sonicleaning and autoclaving surgical
packs, folding blue paper drapes, mopping kennels, scrubbing tissue clumps
    off
hemostats with a toothbrush dipped in chlorhex, these are satisfying, pleasantly
tiresome and when you've done them you can look at the thing and say, it is
    done,
I did that, bolt up a shelf with wall anchors, drill holes for new towel rods, so

now even when you cough ugly insinuations into my inbox *(the reason you are
suicidal is that you know you are too worthless to live)* and complain sarcastically
about my pyrrhic victory—but I don't know what that means, pyrrhic because
you didn't like it that I left? or that you don't know where I moved?—
                                                    now manage

for whole long days to forget about your baby rage, just sit on the concrete
    stoop
staring blankly out into the strange yard, kitty carefully investigates the broken
canes of old rose bushes—then at that second if there is anything much better
    than

eating unwashed blueberries out of the carton in dumb peace,
I have no idea what that could be.

Glitter & plaid.

Three of them are named Katherine, like the year I got dumped twice
in the same parking lot (DeVargas Mall, Santa Fe, New Mexico), it strains
credulity, even when it happens to you part of you doesn't quite believe it,

the theorist says *the queer sixth sense* and you have it even as a tiny girl, watch
Batman while not understanding the difference between kitsch and camp
but knowing what it means when they're tied up writhing like that,

I don't know if the married ones do know. I think they think it'd be
easy, like going to a new restaurant or trying a fun combination of skirt
and blouse so it's up to me to be superheroic, save us from their

unboundaried cluelessness, when I handed her the box of mineral water
in the dark and accidentally backhanded her in the tit did she flinch, I
cringed over it for weeks, do all platonic friendships get watered down

next to the lurid potential my imagination freights, one lives in Estonia
and in Århus, one in Brisbane, one in Newcastle, one in Nebraska, you
can't make this up, two are named Elizabeth. I can't make up

that time when the one letter lost in the post was the hotel reservation
in the purple envelope, can't make up that he used to call me every
time when his wife went out of town, wandering the house in boxers

eating plastic-wrapped cheese with sharp mustard for meals and crying,
can't make up the ferocity that seizes you in the grim local minimum
of the night so roll facedown in bed and bite the sheets but laughing,

he thinks it's facile, that my substituting constellations of beloveds is a
challenge for anyone trying to love me, thinks he knows what I haven't
written: like I'd let fingerprints get all over three hundred pages of angel,

like it's painless to admire her artless selfies (scoop between collarbone
and shoulder, curve of back, slope of neck, basin of attraction), to learn
names of cats and husbands, like it comes naturally to stand down, be

politic and distant instead of shriek beneath her window with lute
tuned to a unison drone, my teacher warned me, you're from another
century, a different economy, you don't think in terms of markets but like

a troubadour, as if pouring all at her feet in a pool would make you more
valuable. But this is capitalism, when you flood the market it makes you worth
less. And I am. Is there a problem with that, no, no there isn't, I've

drawn it down, swallowed hard. Sleep with an arm wrapped around
the hard belly of a guitar like an undergrad. *You don't get to give me education*
is how she shut it down. I told stories to spinneret across space, sketch

an analogous weltanschauung but she informed me otherwise; I just
sound patronizing. She's right. Hey. Listen. I've stopped everything.
Don't cypher anymore. Said I was sorry, nodded tightly and agreed.

Careful to excise the bowerbird's need, delete its gifts. Fold up
the sepia love-letter of misspelled Arabic that she read once, put that
shit away. I button my flannel to the throat. I smile with half my face.

Psych.

I don't change the pillowcases, I don't feed the sourdough starter;
I eat the dog's peanut butter out of the jar with a dirty spoon, I shave one
leg one day, one the next. Look what matters is the things you won't believe,
the sand pink at night with reflected
cloudlight like a neon strawberry Starburst, no one

would believe that, how many times I can come with the right person,
that's unremarkable, how I never throw up, how when I do it's a battle,
all the songs I know the words to, obscure roaring '20s show tunes, everything
the radio has to offer I've worked out all my own harmony parts, and no one
knows. I think of things as bird sizes:

pelican, seagull, plover, sandpiper. That
part's not true. Shrimp boat; cruise ship. That always makes me think of Dave.
That always makes me think of Jeremy, but sometimes I think of me,
myself soaked in urine, me climbing the ladder. If I told him all of this
would he just say, *we need to get you some better peanut butter,*

someone once said to me *Any bed would be immeasurably improved
by having you in it* and I guess my bed-improving days are over,
I definitely cough and tire, I thought all that time I was pretty when all I was
was skinny and young. Or maybe I was something; there's
that picture of us at right angles together and we look like something (can't call
    her bourgeois

because my replacement is a climate activist), look what matters is what
I don't believe, don't bother, remember how you blew it, remember *when
I hear you saying that, I feel like you're a bitch.* I spend ten minutes
thinking about Nervous Nellie and Nosy Parker, why are those
even things, why do I know these things. I spend

an hour thinking about the time my dad tried to start a country
and now he's dead. That part's true. We used to say *psych*, we used to be all like,
grody, I never got to wear the size two black
watch plaid skirt the way it should have been worn, with fishnets and Doc
Martens back when I had a fucking thigh gap. Before Christian Bale, before
    Christian

Slater, before christians there was dad preaching
the gospel of jesus in leather
sandals, a ratty brown beard, a hippie shirt,
the jeans worn long and fringed,
before there was dad i don't know

what there was he was
always there he never left me
alone I was daddy's girl I was in trouble I was
backing away on all fours gasping to
retch the sound of a zipper is not real

the white owl turns her face to you sharply
like the moon, probably I shit, any beach
would be immeasurably improved by having us off it, trampling
dunes and crab tracks by 2050 Iowa cornfields will be the tropics this isn't just
    decoration
we all want to scream all the time now

and sometimes we do. Do you have
an ejection strategy. Can you extract the agent from the field. No one
will ever know my weird high harmony to a pop anthem for which I don't
    particularly
care, that's also not true, I like bad songs. But once in Cambridge
once in a summer dress I rode my

cycle around a bend and the curve was the
arch of the music played, reverberant
steel on an edge, copied, duplicated, echoing. What became of that busker,
you can't get Irish cream ale anymore. They all got married. The dog slumps
    onto his side with
a sigh. I lick the back of the spoon, grow quiet, look stupid out into late autumn

navy-washed night. Hey you know what's magnificent?

East Beach.

The water was brown, brown and the billows
would lift you up and down as if that
was what you wanted, what did you want:
horizon swallow me up, give back my hope,
instead there was nothing to do but float
in that frothy brown bath, warm as a cup
and you can't see the bottom, feel it lift
and drop you, not in a pattern, and some broke
over and slapped you full in the mouth
and that was fine, you spat and shook back
your wet hair and thought *I am a fool not
to do this twice a day*—they surge and grope
your dress, sodden skirt rises, pull it out to let
air bubbles free, gulp, another lurch, opens
below your feet engulfing space filled with god
knows what: weeds and fish and stings, spines
and cuts, keep your eyes on the blurred oil
rigs offshore, dead zone, hypoxic and rank as
we soak and wreck, another one comes, you go up,
up—they slant in staggered rifts, burn skin, strange
bliss—this water is what you waited for, is, is *this*—

NOTES

epigraph—from *Angels* by Denis Johnson (1983) and "We are spirits of another sort" by Whit Merule (2013).

page 4—from "The Reichenbach Fall" by Stephen Thompson (2012).

page 20—from "The Man on the Dump" by Wallace Stevens (1923).

page 27—"Request" is for Jeremy Brent Spohr.

page 31—"I would eat his heart in the marketplace" from Beatrice in *Much Ado About Nothing* (1598); "all men say 'What' to her" from Emily Dickinson (L271, 1862); "my moment of Brocade—/ My—drop—of India" from Dickinson (F388, 1862); "my passionate sisters" and "slovenly needlewomen" from Marina Tsvetaeva, "We shall not escape Hell," tr. Elaine Feinstein (1915).

page 32—"we dressed every morning in / fine Chinese silk, and we would / sing our paradisal songs at / the fire of the robbers' camp," from Tsvetaeva, op.cit.; "My white soprano injuries" from "Radiating Naïveté" in *The Master Letters* by Lucie Brock-Broido (1995).

page 34—from Naomi, Ruth 1:21, tr. Lois C. Dubin (1994).

page 55—from *Antony and Cleopatra* (1606).

page 60—"Operation soul retrieval" is for Jon Davis.

page 70—from *Lolita* by Vladimir Nabokov (1953).

ACKNOWLEDGEMENTS

Much gratitude to the literary journals in which the following poems first appeared: *Cola Literary Review*, "Psych"; *Spoon River Poetry Review,* "Syncope"; *Hampden-Sidney Poetry Review*, "Guttersnipe" and "She's my boyfriend"; "Lucie," *Missouri Review*; "Introduction," "Maere," "Michel," "Kateri," "Maren," "Clarisa," "Rowen," and "Sam," *Michigan Quarterly Review Mixtape*; "In which she makes mistakes by the Mississippi," *Impossible Archetype;* "Kissing girls and left-hand turns," "Dear za'atar," *Q/A Poetry;* "Endemic," *Superstition Review;* "Love song for Rachel," *Sinister Wisdom;* "Blister & filth," "More than one apricot," "Sequin," *Screen Door Review*; "A needle of sapphires & thieves," "Pyrrhic," "Glitter & plaid," *GASHER;* "Dear analogous beloved, or poem," "Diegetic," *Hobart;* "Operation soul retrieval," *DIAGRAM.*

The author would also like to thank Sara Lowe and Elias Lowe, W. Gordon Harris, Gina Palmer and David R. Bates, Penny Gill, Eva Hooker, Margot Backus, Jill McDonough, Katie Schmid, Rachel Malis, Clarissa Springer, Valerie Duff-Strautmann, Naomi Jacobs, Norman Dubie, Tim Ramick, Laura Egley Taylor, C.A. Stamper, Elizabeth Weeks, and my groupchat, Bookclub. There are others I cannot name here but rest assured I still love you madly.

JSA Lowe's poetry chapbook *Cherry-emily* was printed by Dancing Girl Press (2015), and her chapbook *DOE* by Particle Series Books (2012). Her essays have recently appeared in *Denver Quarterly* and *Rupture*. She is an adjunct professor of literature at the University of Houston—Clear Lake, and she lives on Galveston Island.